Dedicated to the inspirational characters that impacted my life and shaped my journey.

I wish you were here to witness how you always empowered my childhood, teenage, and adolescent period of my life, my grandma. Thank you for the unconditional love you pumped in my veins throughout my struggles. I am sure you are in Heaven, blessing my journey.

To my brother, Zouhair, my cornerstone who always believes in me no matter what it takes.

To my friend Sahar, who took me out of darkness to enlighten my life by accepting who I was and who I became.

To the lady who supported me when I struggled again with my beliefs and values and gave me a reason to fight and be strong again…Maram.

To my mom, who never gave up on me and who is a real example of a totally independent successful woman from scratch.

To my dad, who set the real example of serving all people around, make them feel better about themselves and always gave me a vision towards my future.

To those who gave me the first insights – Mahdi, Husam Elias, Abdulrahman, Awfa Mustafa, Nidal, Obaida and Big G, Wardany, Kundan, Steven Green.

To my dream catalyst, Cheryl Chapman, Andy Harrington and my role model, Tony Robbins.

To my mentor Jean-Pierre De Villers, who believed in me, gave me the right tools to reach the peak of my vision and bringing it to life, to the person who answered my request and gave me the opportunity to get ready to manifest my dream.

To all passion seekers, to all change makers, to you who just took the first step towards living a meaningful life.

Hiba El Ayal

The Chemistry of Passion Lab

Step-by-Step Guide to Unleash Your
Happiness Potentials

AUSTIN MACAULEY PUBLISHERS™
LONDON • CAMBRIDGE • NEW YORK • SHARJAH

ISBN 9789948374831 (Paperback)
ISBN 9789948374862 (E-Book)

Application Number: MC-02-01-7825507
Age Classification: 17+

The age group that matches the content of the books has been classified according to the age classification system issued by the National Media Council.

First Published (2019)
AUSTIN MACAULEY PUBLISHERS FZE
Sharjah Publishing City
P.O Box [519201]
Sharjah, UAE
www.austinmacauley.ae
+971 655 95 202

Table of Contents

What Is Passion?

Perhaps you are here because you are feeling incomplete even though you have a great career and a good salary where you can be achieving extraordinary results at your work and yet not satisfied.

Maybe you are living your life on others' terms and conditions, where everything controls your life except you.

Possibly, when you go to bed, every night, you keep on hearing the 'mini-sounds' whispering about another life you want, and not just an existence, so turmoil takes over internally and your battles start because you don't want to wake up in the morning in order to stay in another world you created before you slept.

Potentially, you are experiencing a plateau phase and here nothing matters and you just hide behind a mask of a fake smile or stop reflecting your real emotions.

So, where can you be instead?

Imagine that over here you rise and shine every morning full of energy and you are grateful that you are still alive and full of abundance.

What if here you have this sense of internal peace and you just accept and love being you, where you are extraordinary for yourself and others.

Here, you are a source of inspiration, where everyone around you can feel your vibes and approach you to know the secret behind your awakened, genuine smile.

Here, you only lead a life of significance, which are these rewarding words and feelings you get from your environment and yourself that makes you feel proud.

Now, do you agree with me to move from where you are right now to where you want to be instead you need a new approach?

Albert Einstein says: "Insanity: Doing the same thing over and over and expecting different results."

So, this is why I have created *The Chemistry of Passion Lab* to give you the right tool that will pave the way for you to achieve a self-motivated happy life.

What am I really talking about?

I believe that life is like a roller-coaster where only few would enjoy this journey and others might just stand and watch from a distance behind assumptions and fear and frustrations, hence, time will pass wishing that they embraced the ride.

However, would you recall days that you have done such activities and called it adventurous and now you can't even think about doing this again?

That is why I am inviting you, now, to take a self-discovery journey, it is the ambition materialized into action and the energy force that create a strong feeling of enthusiasm and excitement towards a meaningful life and finding your purpose of living.

This time we will travel inwards and break the blocks that are preventing you from pursuing your passion and unleashing your happiness potential.

Congratulations!!! I can already see that you took the first step towards pursuing your passion because you are here right now and that is why it is my responsibility to strengthen your first decision and tell you why it's important to stay with me and start the chain reaction of the life changing decisions and actions that will accompany you through the coming few chapters in order to create your extraordinary life. It's never late and it's the right time now to enjoy the roller-coaster ride that will help you serve yourself, your community, and even contribute to the world.

So, do you know who really had the same decisions as you have taken right now?

There are many examples; however, I choose three of them who are still impacting our life every day and definitely you know them.

First, Steve Jobs, the ex-CEO of one of the most successful companies in the world today – Apple.

During several interviews, Steve always shared his number one successful principle: "Do what you love," and where Carmen Gallo wrote an article titled 'The *Seven* Success Principles of Steve Jobs', based on an interview with Steve Jobs. In that article he said, "People with passion can change the world for better," so he always claimed that the passion he had for his work made the difference.

Second, Mark Zuckerberg, the young self-made billionaire who changed the world connecting people by Facebook and when he talks about the ingredients of success, it is following your passion and your happiness so even if it doesn't end by making a fortune, you will at least be doing what you love.

Last but not least, Bill Gates who created Microsoft was passionate enough about computers that in the eighth grade, he managed to get excused from math class to design things like early video games.

If Steve, Mark and Bill decided passion journey had such a massive impact in the world, what could you do if you pursue your own passion?

The important thing that there are many examples who took the same journey and put their vision into reality…Yes, I know that is not easy but achievable…and why it's worth doing?

Because you already paid the price of boredom and suffering of where you were before reading this book. Or you are stuck in a phase that you need evidence to take this leap of faith…and it is the only time you take charge over your life and choose a purpose for your living that you would never go out without being excited thinking about it.

Would you like to discover your auto-pilot button that will take you to a higher level of natural adrenaline rush, every day?

Mark Twain says: "The two most important days in your life are the day you are born and the day you find out why."

Obviously, you know when you were born, but do you have any clue of the other important day? Maybe it is today? What if it just happens, now?

No one is certain about the day he will leave this world, the only certain thing that there is a 'Hyphen' between the date you were born and the sad and certain truth that you will pass away.

How do you want your hyphen to look like? How many lives you want to inspire before you go? How would you love to be remembered? What 'legacy' do you want to leave?

Thinking about the answers to these questions is overwhelming. Now the good news is that you don't have to do it on your own. Through the coming chapters you will be guided step by step to get out with a clear, defined passion and an action plan that will serve you in creating the life you desire.

Why This Book Will Unleash Your Happiness Potential?

Maybe you are wondering why to keep on reading and why to follow the system I have created, so let me share with you my story.

If you come back with me to the winter of 1997, on a Monday, you will find me in the mount of Lebanon in my school's playground that is viewing the city of Beirut and the airport, it is very cold and students are playing and it's break time.

With my arms crossed, I am watching airplanes taking off and guess who is taking a flight right now, my mom Jamila. She is a young pretty lady and she looks like Halle Berry.

Why did she leave?

I am always getting high grades in class!

Am I not good enough for her to stay?

What is divorce? And why she left back to Dubai?

All these thoughts are crushing my mind and I don't have a clue about the answers.

Can you imagine, how a ten-year-old child would feel in such a situation?

Couple of weeks later, you will find me on Sunday sitting with my miserable thoughts beside the fireplace in the living room that is full of dark-green couches and a television…The door knocks and I run to open. "Grandma!!!!" She is a huge, tall, old woman, who always wear a black dress.

"So, Grandma, you are going to stay with us?"

"Yes, my lovely, granddaughter. I wish I will live until the day I see you graduating from university."

With Grandma's unconditional love, I was able to face the storm and the only thing I had control of is being an intelligent student at school so I can pursue her dream to see me the first lady to graduate from university in my family.

Days are passing and she became weak for several years…and on 22nd of July 2008, the only heart that pumped for me throughout my life just stops…"One more year and I will graduate."

Have you ever had a time that you lost someone precious to you; a friend, a close relative, or a family member?

This was me…I never imagined that I will lose her one day especially that she filled a huge gap for me during the seven years that I didn't see my mom…yes, I graduated with a bachelor degree in biology…However, it doesn't have a sense when the person who initiated this dream is not there.

Here comes the life of distractions…running to everything that makes me forget, myself, my identity and the good in me…yes, yes, right it is the things that you are thinking of now.

Did you have this period in life that you created your own zone of running away from accepting the fact?

Did you try compensating losses by emotional eating, alcohol, depression, drugs, or whatever…?

Fast forward to the summer of 2011…You will find me in my room on my bed, talking to my imaginary friend, a brown teddy bear called Wilson…where I felt like Tom Hanks in the movie *Cast Away*…when it is the only way he had to communicate on the isolated island he is living in.

My brother arrives for a summer vacation from Dubai…He is a handsome guy, taller than me, a bit with black hair and tanned skin…

"Hiba, what is going on? I am worried about your life…You always inspired me towards being smart and positive, and suddenly I find you in your room with no career? Would you like to come with me to Dubai? There you will start a new chapter and you will find a good job…"

This is the time I decide to grab this chance and move to Dubai…and thank God I did.

I started a corporate career where after one year, my manager Wael, he is a tall white man, did a job rotation, so we, his team, could experience our true potentials.

First, sales manager of the month…done, second, a marketing campaign initiative…it was hectic and I did it.

Here is the thing…when it came to a training initiative…I was totally immersed in this task and worked for endless hours and yet I am feeling so energetic, you will find me reading *The Secret* book in order to teach my team the power of positivity…I would never forget this feeling…however, it was a task and done…but the feeling that accompanied the task never left me.

When was the last time that you stopped for a moment and thought of what makes you happy?

"What do I really want?"

"Where can I give limitless?"

"What is the only thing that will motivate me again?"

"I am fed up…I want to become like Tony Robbins…I want to help people…?"

"Come on Hiba, wake up…no one will listen to you."

Have you ever had this 'mini-you' sounds in your head that keep pulling you back?

I had the same sounds but I decide to get them out and here comes 'BIG G'…I call him 'BIG G' because he is the big hammer that breaks these sounds always…he always served me as if he is a big brother.

On the 15th of December 2016, you will find me with him, in a fancy business lounge in one of the hotels in Dubai. 'Big G' is huge in size with blond hair and has very sharp smart eyes.

"How are you, Hiba? Long time? Tell me what is going on, what achievements have you made since you moved to your new company?"

"Ahhh I'm fine, success, Big G, I am not the lady you know anymore, I am stuck, nothing more motivates me, I feel like a failure…?"

"Wow-wow-wow…What's wrong with you, Hiba?"

"I don't know sometimes I think I want a promotion but this is not the situation…Even if I am the CEO of the company, I will not be happy."

"Okay so what you want to be Hiba?"

"Big G, I have been attending a lot of self-enrichment workshops here and there for three years and if it helped me this much on personal level for sure I can help many other people like me to cope from their losses so I want to become a speaker but I have no clue how to start…and I am afraid I am going to lose my six years' career in pharmaceuticals and don't know if it generates income…?"

"Hey, Hiba, take it easy my friend…Did you forget that you have a great networking skill and know how to approach people successfully??? Do you have a plan??"

"A plan no, Big G, I don't. I just hate planning; we do this at work and you want me to do a plan."

"Have you ever had a time that you felt like you know what works, and you just procrastinate and give excuses??"

"Yes, Hiba, come let me show you an easy way…You need to have this physical plan to visualize what is missing and connect the dots, and why are you wasting time learning from those who aren't leading in this industry don't you know someone who is successful?"

"Oh my God! Yes, yes, last year I attended a workshop for an international successful speaker, his name is JPDV and he gave us his email?"

"Then Hiba do your plan and ask JP for his help, he might reply, you never know…just ask."

On the 22nd of December 2016, you will find me planning and taking action as if it is going to happen.

On 25th of December 2016, on the same day I emailed JP, JP replied back and he is open to help.

Fast forward to 5th of January 2017, you will see me in the Sheraton hotel meeting JP, he is a very tall man, with an athletic body and brown to hazel hair, and his eyes are so blue.

He walks me to the business lounge.

"So, Hiba, you want to be a speaker?"

"Yes…yes…I have a plan but I don't have certificates to do it JP…"

"Oh you don't need any, Hiba…you just have to increase your self-confidence."

"Listen, Hiba, what do you think, if I give you an opportunity to speak on my stage this year? Would you accept it?"

"Yes, yes, yes…"

Richard Branson says: "If someone offers you an amazing opportunity and you're not sure you can do, say yes – then learn how to do it later."

This opportunity got me back to being a student of life, I started enjoying the roller-coaster again…I started preparing and getting ready. I practiced many times…I want to be ready…I quit my 9-5 job…I know what you're thinking, it's a crazy decision, but I had to burn the ship to win the island

Now, I am a certified professional public speaker from Andy Harrington's Professional Public Speakers Academy, after traveling all the way from Dubai to London several times and challenging myself and practicing there a lot.

And on first of April 2017, in a massive hall full of around two hundred people who are hungry to learn and become more, guess who is holding the microphone on stage…Yes it's me introducing JP with high levels of energy to his audience.

Then, the dice rolled and from one stage to another, you will find universities and congresses calling me in order to give influential talks.

Fast forward, I started coaching clients on how to reach their true potentials and give them the right mindset on how to bring passion to their lives and do what makes them be happy.

Now you heard about me and how did I found my pleasure-purpose balance in life, doing what I love to do every day, and let me show you how you can also achieve the same result in order to do what makes you find energy, and live passionately so that is why I have discovered four key elements you need to focus on in order to unleash your happiness potentials.

Why People Fail to Live with Passion?

The four focus areas a passion-seeker like you might focus on to proceed your journey of self-discovery.

First: Aware

The first important step that I have discovered is being aware, now most of my clients at my chemistry of passion lab come to ask me first several questions like: "what is my passion?", "can I really possess one?" and maybe you might ask yourself the same question, and let me tell you this, being aware is a very crucial step. You have to think about it like this if you want to go to a new location you never visited before assigned as point B, what do you usually do? Majority of you will type point B using your navigator, but wait a second will it function without knowing your current location assumed as its point A? Even the best navigator won't get you to point B without the coordinates of point A, you may dwell many years on the wishful thought of happiness and never find it.

It is exactly defining your current potentials 'point A', how does 'A' look like exactly so you can have a clear start button to move in the right direction to reach point 'B'.

Second: Action

In addition to being aware, you have to take action towards your passion.

When I ask many of my clients at the Chemistry of Passion Lab, what do you usually do after work? Most of them say, "Nothing, I just can't wait until I rest from an exhausting day at work," and many others would say, "I just love being at my comfort zone."

But let me tell you something, you can't know what makes you feel happy and simply lay down home after work at your couch watching television and expect that it will come to you at your comfort zone, it is not a comfort zone.

I believe it is a death zone.

Simply, taking the right actions in the right direction is non-negotiable part of reaching your maximum happiness potentials of your passion.

Third: Associate

Now it's important that you are aware and getting into action, but that is not everything; you also need to focus on this part that will either break you or make you? So, how do you 'Associate' your passion? Jack Canfield, number one success coach and speaker on personal growth, says: "You are the average of the five people you spend the most time with."

Look around you, who is in your inner circle? How many times you thought of a new concept and when you express your idea to a close person you just face a huge resistance or they just laugh at it and you pull back from it.

At this phase my clients learn how to grow their plant with the right vital elements like water and sunlight preventing any disease from attacking their happiness and their dream.

You can also learn how to associate your passion with the right elements, like my students do in order to help them gain the right passion accelerators.

Fourth: Amplify

We started by being aware and taking action and even after we associate our actions with the right people and thoughts you also need to 'Amplify'.

A lot of clients I meet, they fulfilled many roles and part of their passion in their lives, however, they reach a level that they get tired, demotivated at a certain level which leads them to give up? So maybe you also faced similar situation. Here you need to amplify and what is it? It is the time where you identify your energy levels and listen to your body triggers and know what strategy to use and when.

Think of it this way, if you are taking a flight you notice that during the take-off period that the captain reduces the light or any energy spending tools in the airplane in order to give the engine the maximum power to take off and reach a steady phase in the sky, then you should have a transit phase to re-fuel.

When you learn how to amplify your thoughts and actions, you will be able to keep pushing beyond what you ever experienced and gain tolerance in order to be a happy person.

The Pleasure-Purpose Finder

This a journey of massive actions that I complied from what worked for me during my past three years that will also shape your destiny. It is all there in you, my system will lead you in the extraction process of the 'new' you as it did for many of my students.

First: Aware

Here, in order to be more focused in being aware, I have to introduce you to two systems 'The Brain Mapping System' and 'The Personality Investigation Pipeline'.

A) The Brain Mapping System

When you were born, you start growing up absorbing your passive understanding to your own unique experiences and your beliefs piles up from school, friends, family the environment around you, it builds up your own map in your brain and the brain loves to save its energy by jumping to assumptions, so everyone of you, including me, had a series of significant emotional events or a trauma in their lives, that results in carrying it with you in any future experiences by creating a certain way of reacting towards life events. Where are you today? It is time to question your beliefs, at this point you will stop few moments with yourself to imagine that you are taking out your brain to start a dissection process that will enable you to understand the cause root of your behaviors today and how to keep the beliefs that serves you and eliminate the excess baggage.

1. Beliefs

Beliefs are the feelings of certainty about the ideas, thoughts, and meanings that you attach to your identity and it's embedded in your mind that guides you in perceiving your surroundings and influences your daily interactions with everything. So, what idea do you have about yourself today? Why do you do what you do? What stops you from moving forward? What meaning have you attached to any previous event of your life?

This is the start button, now, that will serve you understand what do you know about yourself. Here, you will experience two types of beliefs:

a) Limiting beliefs: it is the idea or the meaning you attached to an experience that limits your progression and holds you back. What is the story you tell yourself when things don't work as you expect? Do you feel 'not good enough'? Do you feel like a 'failure'? Do you feel afraid of the 'unknown'? Do you blame yourself? Do you fear being alone or abandoned? Do you feel unworthy?

b) Empowering beliefs: it's the words and meanings you attach to your previous life experiences that made things work for you even on your worst days, what you told yourself those days. How did you lift yourself up? Did you consider failure as a normal part of learning and didn't give up? How did you feel good enough and worthy?

So, let's do a simple exercise, you only need a pen, a mirror and be in a place that you're not disturbed and you!!

The importance of this exercise is the time you be brave, and tap into yourself, and be honest with yourself because the truth will set you free, you have to understand that this is a judgment free zone, no blaming, no sufferings, no guilt, you already had enough time to suffer before being here.
Ready!!!

Activity:

1) Take a slow deep breath till four seconds, hold it for six seconds then exhale, do it for several times.
2) Look into your eyes in the mirror, look at yourself for four minutes, it is you versus you.
3) Now, take some time to fill in the following sheet.

What limiting belief you have?	What is the cause behind it?	What is it costing you today?

2. Behavior

Everyone has developed his own internal pharmacy to handle the beliefs you have, it leads you to behave the way you do today, so your beliefs results in a certain pattern of actions towards future events, so it is the tip of the iceberg you see above the underlying beliefs. According to your beliefs you have developed your own ways to cope and feel that you are on track, these are called patterns, for example some people start smoking or emotional eating, and gain weight as a result, gets frequently angry, procrastinate, experience anxiety and many other behaviors, this happens without paying attention. Do you notice any pattern in the way you are behaving?

Basically, there are four types of patterns that you might experience:

a) Controller: it is the pattern one may develop that is associated emotionally and tends to control everything around, for example a divorced father would tend to control siblings life in an extreme manner, control decisions in a team, control life partners etc., however, at some point this behavior will affect his/her family life, especially career wise because a controller won't succeed with leading a team.

b) Pleaser: here one may develop a pattern to please everyone around, this is the way one may feel good about himself, and may conflict later on with the inner happiness because saying yes to everything or everyone else won't leave you with time for yourself and you tend to please all persons around instead of yourself.

c) Computer: this pattern is developed by letting a person dissociate from his feelings, thinking that the same situation won't happen from him so he/she watch for example a car accident from a distance without imagining that it would happen to him/her. Computers lack empathy which is a basic skill for human interactions.

d) Distractor: this is a pattern, that wears procrastination as its favorite dress, an individual here, also would be emotionally dissociated from his/her feelings, and for example you will find them changing topics while discussing certain subject at work, you may also find them doing everything else except the task that is required for work, etc.

Another simple exercise here will help you bring out the unconscious actions into the conscious reality. According to what you have filled in the previous exercise identify how you react according to your limiting beliefs.

Previous mentioned limiting belief	Unwanted behavior as a consequence of it

3. Break

It is time to break the chain between the beliefs and behaviors to build new perceptions about yourself. You have to understand that your brain believes anything you keep on telling it. It doesn't have the capability to differentiate if it's true or not. I will list several tips that will work for you. You can choose the method that feels right for you and practice it.

a) *The Law of Reaping*

If you plant any idea, it will grow to manifest its nature, what I want to say is that if you keep holding on the limiting beliefs you have you will keep on getting the same result from.

So the first way here, is to stand a guardian on the door of your mind, pay attention consciously to what you are allowing yourself to believe and choose your thoughts, like choosing the best ingredients for your best plate.

b) *Self-acceptance*

Whatever idea you hold about yourself, now it's time accept it, you have tried so hard holding on your past thoughts so what would you lose if you don't resist it anymore, denial, sadness, anger and worrying won't end until you accept what is going in your life. It's not your fault anymore, anything that you experienced before you should accept and let it go.

You have to think about it like this, imagine you have a knife in your hand the more you hold on it the more it's harming you, and always amazing things lies on the other side of letting go. No one is perfect, yet you can raise your standards and step up to allowing yourself to make mistakes.

The past is not your home, it is a place you refer to only for the lessons you learnt…you live in the 'Now' house that is the present.

So, the prescription you can use here is to start using affirmations like:

"I am good enough."
"I love myself and love is everywhere."
"I am worthy."
"I am successful."
"I am healthy."
"I am wealthy."

Write them on a white paper and stick it to your washroom mirror, so in the morning these would be the thoughts you feed your subconscious mind with that serves as an autopilot and it will guide you throughout the day to make your affirmations happen.

c) *The Dickens Process*

This is a method I love because Tony Robbins, the world leading life coach, uses it in his seminars, and I tried it personally, get your pen out and fill in the blanks, I suggest you take it in a calm place because I believe this one will be a turning point in your life if you give it the right attention, the point here is that to associate enough pain with a belief you have so the brain gets motivated to change it.

Exercise

Breathe in and exhale slowly.
Choose two of the above limiting beliefs that you have written in the first table, and answer the following questions:
Now,
How much they weigh you in this life? What did it cost you in the past and now? Stop and think about it.
Feel the loss...Pain is Present. What does it costs you financially? Did it stop you from taking risks? Do you feel powerful or weak? Do you feel energy? What do you say to yourself when you look in the mirror having these beliefs? Tell yourself how do you feel? Is it the model you want your children to look for? Is it the how you want your colleagues to see you? How are these affecting all areas of your life today?

____

____

____

____

____

____

Take the weight and step 5 years in future and take it with you to your future,

What are the feelings it is causing you? Is it more frustration, anger, pain? What are the things you given up? Five years later in the future, how will you look like? Look at your face in the mirror, are you alive or energized? What happened to your self-esteem? What price you paid? Did these beliefs caused you more weight and distractions with food, smoking? Did you miss your career? What is it costing you with your connections?

____

____

____

____

____

____

____

Take the same weight with you 10 years forward,

Is it disappointing? How do you feel? Heavier or lighter? Stronger or weaker? Ten years, a decade with the same beliefs, what did you give up emotionally? What did it cost you on your relationships? Did you give up your level of passion? How do your friends think of you? Feel the pain with the same limiting beliefs, write your feelings down.

____

____

____

____

____

____

Now imagine taking the same weight with you twenty years forward,

How will your face and body look like? Are you more excited or totally depressed? Again what is it costing you? What you didn't try? How will your family life look like? What do say to yourself? Are you living with worry? If it is not painful enough, ask yourself questions until you feel the pain

____

____

____

____

From this point come backwards till today, still nothing of all the preceding happens, you are still alive now shake your body, change your state, breathe and break all the patterns…move again and breathe more and speak loud, and write down the two limiting beliefs, cross them then write down the two new empowering ones, for example : old limiting belief : "I am not good enough"(to be crossed) the new empowering one, "I am the one who approves myself and as long as I am alive I am doing my best and nothing is perfect."

I just gave you an example you can choose to write anything that you feel it empowers you.

Old limiting belief	New empowering belief

If you have done these exercises, I congratulate you because you will notice how life will take you to another level from now on to notice the space you have cluttered for new things to happen to you, I would advise you to share your new empowering belief with someone you trust or send it to me on my social media presence, celebrate yourself and I am going to celebrate you also…On the other hand, if you didn't do it, I am afraid that the rest of the book won't benefit you until you put the work that is required because the key to change is taking action with the exercises I am providing you.

B) The Personality Investigation Pipeline

It is not only your beliefs that you have to be aware of to take charge over your happiness, it is also your personality and where you stand today in all life aspects that you have to dig in in order to create pleasure and purpose in life. I believe that there is no size fits all, because there is nothing called luck or talent, you can learn or do or be any person you are, anything you practice in life you master. The point of this part is to support you raise awareness around you in three different aspects that might be creating a source of struggle in your life to help you upgrade your standards in life.

a) *Identity*

I believe that all personality tests are good. However, it might not serve you because you tend to label yourself according to the way you show up in this world and not your real identity and potentiality. On the other side, it is beneficial to know what motivates you as a person, what is this force that drives you to a better life in all aspects. Here, I would refer back to the six human needs of Tony Robbins model.

Certainty	Uncertainty /variety	Growth
Love /connection	Significance	Contribution

If you really understand your needs and the way to fulfill it in a healthy way, you will be able to plan your life events accordingly, depending on your higher two needs.

Certainty, variety, significance, and connection are the four primal needs for any human being and once they are matched, you may feel that you want either to learn a new thing or to give what you have or know, this is where growth and contributors are positioned as the spiritual needs.

1) Certainty

It is the need to feel, secure, safe in control from the present moment towards the future, seeking ease and comfort, and avoiding pain, stress, and risks.

2) Uncertainty

It is the need to have a variety throughout your daily experiences or even surprises. You tend to take risks, and your excitement comes from challenging your emotional, physical, and intellectual being.

3) Love/Connection

You tend to feel worthy by feeling loved and having personal connections that supports your desire to feel alive, it could be an intimate relationship, a friendship, a family bond, or even a relationship with God. It is the need for meaningful relationships.

4) Significance

It is one of the fundamental human needs to feel significant, self-important and wanted. It is very important to know that your happiness comes from practices that make you feel special and important.

5) Growth

If you want to add more pleasure and you are driven by growth, you will always be looking to develop a skill you have, a relationship, a business you are in or even learn new things as part of self-development.

6) Contribution

Contribution is a spiritual need. It emerges from the desire to give value and serve others so in return you experience fulfillment.

Note: Sometimes when we are not aware of our six human needs, we tend to fulfill them unconsciously in an unhealthy way. I just want you to take a few moments to stop here and chose two top needs and reflect on how you used to pursue your two top needs, and how you will replace them with new healthy habits.

For example, I used to seek love and connection with the wrong group of people, and now I found that I can still get the amount of love and connection bond with the right community that helps me grow.

Your top need number one: ___________________________

How did you fulfill it?

____

How and with what you will replace it?

____

Your top need number two: ___________________________

How did you fulfill it?

____

How and with what you will replace it?

____

b) Value

There is nothing better than understanding yourself and this time you will cover knowing your self-worth. You have to think about it like this: Imagine yourself as a manager and you are interviewing a subordinate who is about to get a job position in your team, ask yourself: "Why I have to employ this person specifically?" You have to see the value that this person will add to your team, but let me tell you this, this subordinate is you. What I mean is that how would you brand yourself to you as a manager of your life. I am talking about your set of strength points and talents you have mastered in life and spotlight it, these are your assets that you will remind yourself with once you are in a valley period of your life and the next questions to ask is that what are your skills that you can improve to go back to the peak period of your life? Briefly, what is the world getting when it is getting you?

Exercise: List five strength point you have or skills set you mastered, if you doubt yourself I would suggest that you go and ask five people from your coworkers and family members and friends, this is 'The Confidence List' that you will refer back to and remember it whenever you feel less confident

1. ______________________________________

2. ______________________________________

3. ______________________________________

4. ______________________________________

5. ______________________________________

c) Passion

It is not enough to only understand ourselves, the most important after knowing your true potential is to find what makes you come alive. This is what truly matters because Howard Thurman, who played many leading roles in social justice movements, says: "Don't ask yourself what the world needs – ask yourself what makes you come alive and then go do it."

Perhaps you already know what gets you a strong inclination towards doing a certain activity with enthusiasm and pleasure or maybe you still didn't find it, now my advice is if you still did not find your passion, don't settle, just keep on searching for what makes you feel pleasure, don't give up on finding it, because if you don't at least give a try how would you know it? Time will pass anyway. So, how do you choose to live your life?

This is a simple tip that might uncover your passion so take some time to fill in the blanks:

'The Passion Definer'

1. Write down two of your strength points, you might have listened your friends or clients telling you "you have a unique characteristic doing this…and that…" (Example: energy, care, analysis etc.)

_____________________   _____________________

___   ___

2. How do you really enjoy expressing these two unique characteristics while dealing with your surrounding environment? (Example: to spread, to teach)

_____________________   _____________________

___   ___

3.What will your qualities and giving it to your community ?Write three sentences that describes the way the society or your environment will look like, using to preceding words you used.

____

____

____

____

If you already know it, it is time to start practicing your passion, allocate even if one hour every two week and let it be your zone of pleasure, do it out of enjoyment, if it is really your passion you will sense that the time you work on it flies and you also get a natural adrenaline rush from it. You may try different several activities to find it, the most important thing is that you don't settle because this is the only thing that will give you a strong inclination of feeling towards accomplishing more of it.

The good news is that you can also be aware and consciously do your daily task with passion, which means from all of your heart, add your feelings to it and notice how you are going to drive more pleasure to whatever you're a doing.

Second: Action

I want to salute you now because you have opened up to a new level of consciousness, now that you have a clear understanding of your inner self and got aware of where are you standing today, it is time to start taking action out of what you have usually done on a daily basis, and take new actions in the direction of what really creates more pleasure in your life.

For this reason, I have created the following two systems that is very important and simple to digest at the same time.

1) The Powerful Positioning Practice

Now I would like to ask you a very important question, have you ever asked yourself what makes the brain reach a certain destination? It is essential to understand that your mind always needs clarity over the final destination you desire to reach it whether it is an emotional or physical one, this is why you need to understand the power of creating images and plans that will help you visualize the purpose you are here to fulfill or the needs you want to satisfy.

A) Picture

This is the board where you will just simply draw two phases of your life, relax you don't need to be Picasso to take this exercise, you can feel free to draw or sketch anyway you need to symbolize the action or the state you want to be, however before taking this exercise, you have to know one fact, regardless of any challenges you are facing in order to reach your purpose. According to science and neurolinguistic programming your brain cannot differentiate between what is real and what is imaginary, it believes anything that it visualizes and will support your daily mind function in order to achieve the phase that you will draw on the other side.

Feel free to draw your own sketch or you can utilize photos from magazines on a separate board, cut them, and stick them.

Exercise:

Vision Board Picture

Phase one	**Phase two**
Draw how does your life look like today, and include your emotions on it Ex: Your house, your family, your work, Your relationship with God, your bank account, etc.	Draw how would your life look like in the same aspects you used in phase one, without any limiting, imagine that you have achieved the life you desire and draw it How does it look like and where would you be?

B) Purpose

A wise man once said: "When the intention is clear, the mechanism will appear." What does it really mean? Have you ever seen a child with his parents when he wants something he just keeps on nagging and crying and screaming until he gets what he wants, now I used this example not to tell you to cry or nag, but to tell you that when you know your purpose in life, you just have to hang on it and never let it go, until it happens.

Here, I would remind you of the importance of knowing your 'why' clearly in life, because when life moves in the direction you want it, you want give away fulfilling your needs, but what would keep you going and never giving up in challenging times? When you feel that you just don't have to power to proceed or simply you lose sight over your happiness? It is reminding yourself of your purpose and this is called delaying the gratification mechanism, yes you may understand what you do in life and how it is done, however taking the route of why you are doing it is a better starting point that creates the driving force inside out towards the results you want to manifest in life.

Exercise

Grab a pen again and take few deep breaths and write down your ultimate purpose in life, why you want to do whatever you want today? What is the reason you want to feel proud of yourself? Why you want to wake up from bed every day? Why do you go to work, even when you don't feel like going? Keep the money reason a bit away and dive deep into your spirit. Is it your children, is it your dream, is it yourself.

Go ahead and write your 'WHY'.

____

____

____

C) Plan

Imagine yourself in a kitchen for the first time and you want to cook for guests you are having tonight, first you have to plan what do you want to cook, then you have to do the grocery and get the ingredients of your dinner, after that you will start cooking and know exactly the time it takes your food to be ready, so you can ensure that you have a great evening with your guests.

On the other side, if you didn't plan it well, you will fail to please your guests and may end up getting fast food or any delivery meal.

Now, imagine these guests are you and you are planning your future, if you want to pursue your passion and happiness, you should have a written plan to proceed with the details of your journey, because if you fail to plan, it means you are planning to fail.

Exercise

Write down your goal within the coming three years in the first row, be specific as much as you can.

What do you have? First pillars	What do you need? Second Pillars	Resources to use. Third Pillars	Strategy versus time. Fourth Pillars

2) The Dare to Dream Investor

Perhaps you always had a dream or an idea and planned it well and still, you didn't proceed to the next level of execution because maybe you lacked resources of time and money or even the courage to pursue your purpose, basically this is the time you will need The Dare to Dream Investor's mindset.

How can you create it and what do I mean? I will take you through the steps that will help you comprehend it.

A) Desire

Imagine with me that you are a fan of watching movies and recently, you started hearing people everywhere talking about how amazing is this movie, for sure you will get excited to see it and you will create time even if you have a busy, book a ticket and see it. What if you will have the same feelings, but this time towards implementing your plan, won't you be curious and excited towards the events of your life movie?

This is exactly the desire, I am talking about, you can't move forward in unleashing your happiness potentials without a strong craving that will pull you towards the future.

The exercise here is to tell yourself every day and train your mind, when you have a low energy period to say one magical word: "What if?"
So next time if you catch yourself into an interesting experience, and your mind is trying to bring you down because of fear, just train yourself on the word: "What if?"

Think about the possibilities that may happen if you overcome your fear & step forward

And you will never be able to judge a movie if you don't watch it yourself and enjoy every moment till you reach the end of it.

B) Anchor

It is not enough to only create a desire towards finding a purposeful life, I believe that you need to Anchor this desire with certain things that will provide you certainty in times when you lack confidence in your life.

Here is an example to elaborate more on anchoring, let us say that you have a huge desire to quit smoking, and everyone tells you that you will never do because the majority of smokers don't quit, so what do you do in this case ?

First, after you set the intention of quitting, you have to start keeping a gum next you so once you have the urge to smoke, you can grab a gum instead, I am not telling that this will make you quit but it will start in creating the time you need a cigarette to switch gradually to taking a gum instead.

Another example is when you have certain project in your mind and you would love to take action, you can anchor this habit by choosing a 'goal buddy', who is a person that you trust and he is accountable of encouraging you and following up with you in order to start taking micro-steps towards you, this person doesn't necessarily need to be working on the same project to you he might be achieving his objectives in his own industry, this way you keep yourself anchored to induced motivation.

Now, because anchoring is so important I would love to give you a third example that will show you its importance. Here, consider losing weight and you are not able to hit the gym, but when you hire a coach, this person will keep you anchored to the gym because his job is to train you for one hour every day to reach you objectives of getting a fit body.

So, If you find yourself hesitant about any idea that you know if you pursue it will bring pleasure to your live, simply invest in a life coach who is known for helping people achieve their goals and that what I personally did in order to learn, grow and feel happy achieving career and life objectives on my terms.

In our world today, there are also thousands of applications in your phones that will act as a reminder of taking action and keep record of your progress.

C) Rituals

This is the part that I love because it is the part that will build up who you become, it's the rituals that you practice every day…because what you practice daily, you become.

Rituals are the group of actions you do regularly at least five or six times over the seven days of week.

So if you notice how athletes became who they are, it is by training regularly and keep them self-ready for the next challenge or game.

The importance of rituals is that on days that are very challenging they serve you as

Generally, there are a list of rituals that you can pick up from that almost all successful and happy people practice every day until you find your own and create your own ones:

1) Journaling: we experience a lot of emotion fluctuations during the day and sometimes it is difficult to find someone to really understand us, so a good way of releasing emotions that gives you a sense of relief is downloading all your thoughts, no matter what they are about, on a piece of paper. You might feel afraid that someone would read them, you can simply tear the papers after you finish. What is necessary is to clear space from our mind to be able to allow new space for new experiences and new ideas.

2) Read: Books are the places where you could travel in time and cumulate the knowledge you need in pursuing your purpose in life. It is important that once you set a goal or an objective in your life that you go search for books relevant to the subject, why because simply success leaves clues, you will be able to know, how people before you did it and learn from their mistakes so you could save yourself time and energy that

you could invest in the right direction. You can read one page a day, remember always create micro-wins to persist and persevere by the end of the year you will have a three hundred sixty-five pages done, small actions count and accumulate to collaborate to the huge success you are looking for, and here I define success as living your life on your own terms and feel happy with it.

3) Pro act: Every day choose consciously to control one reaction towards your life events that is going on, because this is the way you will train and ground yourself to grow the muscle of self-control over multiple situations so you will create an unshakeable belief system that will not collapse easily. I believe that you could control any outcome if you will be able to control yourself. This will reduce the level of stress poison you drink during the day and you will be able to reach a good level of stress free life. It is how you choose to react that determines your quality of life every day.

4) Reminders: Create sticky notes with quotes that inspires you everywhere you go and stick them beside your bed, at your office desk, or even set it as your smart phone background. You are a human being and it is natural that you tend to forget things especially at a level where you are still feeling that the results you are looking for are non-tangible, so you never know how these quotes will pop up and remind you with your purpose in life and help you overcome certain challenges in life.

5) Empty your Cup: Your mind subconsciously tends to always give you reasons to feel worried about tomorrow's plan. So here is what I have for you, it is a practice I personally love, because it made my life easier and I wasn't worried about forgetting tasks I want to do in the morning or the next day. So, before you sleep get a paper and write down every single task you need to do the next day, so when you jump in bed you feel safe and feel certain over the flow of the next day and you will relax and get a sound sleep. It is a good way of planning your week track your accomplishments day by day.

D) Enrichment

When I started The Dare-To-Dream Investor, I intended to show you how self-investment is the wealthiest action you can serve yourself with, it might not show results on the same day but you will thank God over the coming years that you took action and proceeded with a huge desire and created your own rituals that will help you create your own protocol in life, but this is not enough, you have to start investing in workshops also.

Allow me to explain the rationale behind this segment through a story that I always remembered before I registered in any workshop that was relative to my dream...A farmer usually plants seeds and he wakes up every morning and invests in his time, money, and effort to go and water the seeds he planted...The interesting fact is with those farmers who grows plants that takes months until they start growing into a shoot that appears above the surface of the soil...Now, surprisingly is that how could this farmer stay patient and never gives up for all this period before he visualizes that shoot of the plant...It is because he by knowledge and experience have seen other farmers before doing the same thing and saw that this plant after months when it rises above the surface it grows then quickly.

The moral of the story is that you want to possess a farmers mindset when you want to grow your dream and engage yourself by booking a seat at least every month or quarter in order to put yourself with the people who did what you are looking for before you and learn from them.

Enrichment here is the key, the action her is to go online now, type the keywords of the workshop that you will find answers in, even if you have to travel abroad this is the greatest asset you are going to invest throughout your life.

Third: Associate

Now, if you are sitting next to me now and you reached this part, I would shake hands with you and celebrate the new you that is emerging by complying with reading this book. I want to tell you that you are on the right track and stay with me because so far after we covered two important sections that are being aware and taking action and also now I will reveal a very essential part that will decide if you are going to stay on track of unleashing your happiness potential by finding your pleasure and purpose in life, it is how you will associate your purpose with.

There are three pillars here that you will identify, through The Safe Vaccination Shield:

1) Circles

In your daily life you have friends, family, and colleagues at work around you, these are the people who influence your life and who will you be.

Whether it is a friend, a colleague, a co-worker or a family member make sure that you manage your expectation from them because most of the disappointments and pain happens at this level.

It doesn't mean if you are biologically related to your family that they will support you on finding your happiness or support you on pursuing a dream or even be on your side with any move you are going to make in the future that might be for a crucial step in your life, and why I am telling you this is because they don't see what you see and you have to take full ownership over your happiness and your responsibility is to keep going and show them that there is another of living your life. In addition to that you gave to stop expecting from them that they would be the first to lift you up and this also applies to any person close to you even if they are your best friends.

So, your mission here is to always know who you are dealing with and manage your expectations so that is why you will have to categorize any person in your life into the following:

A) Family members: These are the people who for a reason God chose them for you to be with them your entire life, in any form, a father, a mother, a brother, a sister, a husband, a wife or siblings etc…so you don't have to expect from them any change to happen or shift in their beliefs towards you or what you are trying to do, your job here is just to love them and accept them as they are.

B) Friends: They are the individuals that you again don't need to expect from them anything and they simply give flavor to your life so you can go out with them, have fun whenever you need a break from life. Don't try to push your ideas or waste energy influencing them with any of your philosophies in life because your job is to set an example and take action simply because people don't care what you say they only care how do you make them feel and with the results that your seeking in life.

C) Supporters: (Inner circle) This person might be a family member, a close friend or a mentor or a coach or any person who you genuinely see their care in you and in believing in your potentials and you can feel that they possess the wisdom or the results you are looking for in life, the most important thing in this bond is the mutual that trust you have between you both. This is the backup system that will run the software of being yourself with them and putting your hero aside to be able to empty your cup of emotions to them.

D) Goal Buddies: It is very essential to search and choose a person who is ambitious towards a certain goal in his or her life to enrich your experience, no matter what the goal is if it is career objective, a spiritual one or a physical one so you can both check on each other from time to time and track their progress and the goal buddy in return also keeps on checking and reminding you on achieving your purpose and not to settle.

Your exercise here is to write down the name of the people around you and list them under the category that is relevant to your experience with them and remember always manage your expectations so you can reduce the disappointments span whenever needed.

Exercise

Family	Friends	Supporters	Goal Buddies

Now after we explained the first pillar, let's go to the second pillar of the Safe Vaccination Shield:

2) Choices

Throughout your entire life you might have always judged any new experience or action that you are willing to pursue because of a significant emotional event that is associated with this action that happened before and programmed yourself not to do it because it was associated with a painful feeling.

These painful feelings for sure lie within the following two feelings that I will explain it later in this part. However, before that I want to bring awareness to the power of making a choice because all the decisions that you will take after depends on these emotions and it is important for you to read it carefully since it depends on building your confidence and trust in your abilities in your choices.

A) Fear of Rejection

After we pass through a certain experience that caused a loss of a friendship a family member or a job or any loss you have encountered, you start to have certain emotions associated with this loss that starts running like a movie and reminds you that because of the event 'X' you have done it caused the 'Y' loss in your and thus it will build a fear of being rejected by your beloved ones that you definitely don't want to repeat again life so unconsciously you start avoiding any new experience that might remind you of a potential loss in the future so over here you start bouncing back to your current state without enduring the fear of rejection that pops up into your mind.

How to counteract this idea is to first be aware of the feeling and the event that is related, then try to find a way in dealing with similar situations in the future by being honest to yourself and know that it is never your fault if you have done everything that you can in order to be rejected. Finally, let me share with you an interesting news that the thing that you're searching for might be on the other side of this fear so conquer it by knowing that you are good enough and taking charge over your actions and trusting the process by moving a step forward.

B) Fear of Judgment

The other choice that you could make in life might be based on either judging yourself or might be based on other judging you as a failure or mean or crazy or money chaser or any idea that you are afraid to perceive from other. However, I will not count for you how many great individuals in history that have been judged for the same ideas and they didn't allow it to put them down or stopped them from achieving greatness. Stop overthinking your image and get out of your head and allow the gifts that you have to be passed to the world by being you. No one have lived your story or faced the challenges or traumas you had in order to judge you properly. Plus when it comes to your personal judgment on yourself don't forget that we are programmed and conditioned to think in a negative way as much as we grow up because it's easier for the mind to save energy and jump to conclusion and find an excuse for what happens. Life doesn't come with a catalogue to say what is right or what and what is wrong, everything is relative in life and based on the period you are experience. Life is just made to be lived fully.

Your exercise here is simply whenever any judgment come to your mind on the way or looking or how you are perceived based on an action that you have taken, tell yourself one more magical word: 'Maybe'.

"Maybe their opinion is right or wrong" or even "Maybe my opinion might be right and wrong".

It is not your job to figure it out, your job is just to accept yourself and seek a way to grow based on the learning you extract from it.

Let's go now to the third pillar of The Safe Vaccination Shield:

We have explained the roles of your circles and relationships that takes place within the circles and also the ideas and fears that are a result based on the interactions that happens day to day in your life. It time to create a network of people that will grow your happiness, business or guide you through the process of pursuing your mission and purpose in life.

3) Connections

Here I am not talking about friendship, or the circles that we mentioned before, here I want to help you get out of your regular comfort zone of individuals that are regularly there in your life. I am speaking about the people how are not present in your daily life because nothing will change with the same circles you know every day you have to expand beyond that and expand your network because as know your network is your net-worth.

If you are not happy in the place you are right now at your work, you can after you set your goals go to the right places or workshops or seminars to cultivate new relationships that might be potentials business partners or investors or new employers. You can monthly build a new base with getting to know at least four or five people that might recommend you or recommend someone to you to help you be in the place that you would love to be.

If you are seeking better finances for example you can also be specific and start interacting in networking events with people who has impressive finances and learn from them how you could enhance yours.

If you are seeking a good life partner, start networking in places who could potentially have more single individuals that holds the likeminded character you are seeking. You never know, I am being totally honest and openly speaking about this part because again everyone has a purpose in life and it could be anything not necessarily a career or a money related goal.

Fourth: Amplify

Currently, you have accomplished the first three integral parts of the step by step guide to direct your mindset in the journey of unleashing your happiness potential and cheer up you have done well so far and stayed committed to explore your pleasure and purpose in life. It is time to reveal the last big chunk of the system which will keep you on track and it is called 'The Recharging S.P.A Retreat'.

I know now you might be picturing the spa where you get the relaxing massages…However, this is not the one I am talking about, more or less it will have the similar feeling by creating a SPA zone in your head through three metaphoric muscle that we will grow together to rest, energize and gain back your motivation level back to its peak level.

Your consisted of three elements the spirit, the body and the mind. As long as you are living and in the act of pursuing your dream or living passionately, you have to take care of 'You'.

1) Spirituality

Your soul needs feeding as you do with your body when you feel hungry, and the question is how will you feed your soul and with what? The answer is simple: to keep the connection with your spirit regardless of what you believe in. You might be religious, so the way to stay connected with your spirit is to keep the bond with the higher spirit like God that you believe in through prayers. It will help you cleanse your soul and gives you certainty over the stormy periods through your life where you might feel angry, which is a high arousal state where your body would react forgetting that the soul could have a power over the situation.

You can also practice meditation that will give you power to be present in the moment and this also give a break to your soul to result in some peaceful moments. It might be difficult at the beginning however the best option is to go for guided meditations many times to start mastering this practice.

This part is all about inspiration and if you break the word it will be the state of being in spirit. It is a simple way to focus on a deep breathe to remember that you are alive. From here you will get the insights and your soul will be nourished.

2) Physical

Following the discussion about the spirit, we have to go to talk about the second part – your body. Your body is the tool that will support you on getting the energy to pursue your passion. If the tool doesn't work effectively, nothing will be accomplished. It is all about energy; it is like the petrol that you fill in your car daily on your way to your work so you could run the engine. So in the case, you will get energy from two things the food you eat and the movements you make. If you feel that you worked so hard for a long period of time and you feel tired, stand up jump five times and tell me how you feel. Definitely, you will feel better now I am not telling to go do a one hour workout in the gym, it is only a few minutes' jumps that will change your total biochemistry of your body and release the endorphins that are the happiness hormones. I don't like to speak about fitness and nutrition because it is not within my areas of expertise, but I would advise you to move, dance, and jump, run…Do what is relevant and easier to you and just move to generate this fantastic spark that will help you feel your body and rush the adrenaline to your brain.

3) Attitude

First was the spirit, then the body and let's go to the mind. All what I have shared with you since the beginning of this guide would be meaningless without this last part that is your attitude. The secret of life lies within this part, it is the key that will unlock your happiness potentials forever and the moment you forget it, you will go through a blame, anger, or a sequence of negative events. It is the attitude of gratitude.

Maybe you heard a lot this word 'Gratitude', and you never really had a chance to understand this terminology and experience it. It is very easy for you on good days to feel grateful for the good events that might happen in your life, and so difficult for you to remember it on days that are hard, challenging, and full of negative events. Gratitude is an everyday job. I am sure you are familiar with the word 'Thank you' and now it is time to dissect this word and feel that value of thanks and who to thank.

You might have passed through a lot of events and still will experience many of them that might not look pleasant and here if you ask yourself one question: "What if what is happening is preparing you for what you have been asking for?" And we all agree that there are no absolutes in life, there is always one good point at least in anything unpleasant event that happens. At least if there is no reason that you could find gratitude for, in such situation you are gaining endurance. Endurance is the ability to endure difficult situations without giving up. I believe that at some point in life you will need this ability even if you don't see its importance and insignificance, why? Because simply life is never a straight line, there is always surprises and days where you feel at your peak and other days you feel at the bottom.

Imagine with me how would your life be, if you are appreciating yourself, your friends, your breath, your heartbeats…Pause for a second and in the days where you feel intense events, put your hands on your heart and take a deep breath in and feel your heart beats. This will remind you that nothing matters as long as you are still alive, there is always a lesson to learn.

The last exercise that I always keep as a main ritual in my life and it saves me a lot from darkness is:

Write down five things that you would like to thank yourself, God or an experience or someone for being the reason you gained something on the other side even if this lesson is very expensive.

Gratitude Exercise

1) ____

2) ____

3) ____

4) ____

5) ____

I would love to offer you now a very unique interactive chance, if you feel you would like to share your gratitude list with me, feel free to email on admin@hibaelayal.com. I would love to hear more about experiences that you felt grateful for and shaped your journey.

Magical Pills

I am so grateful to you for reading my book. Your contribution has made my journey of happiness real. It is because of you that I have compiled all the teachings that I spent three years investing time in in order to simplify the knowledge and tell you that there is always a roadmap for whatever you want to achieve in life in a magical pill. I would love to summarize all what I have experienced with me in my humble system through quotes from people who have created legacy on earth throughout history.

Magical Pills

1) "If I have the belief that I can do it, I shall surely acquire the capacity to do it even if I may not have it at the beginning."

– Gandhi

2) "Never give up on what you really want to do. The person with big dreams is more powerful that the one with all the facts."

– Albert Einstein

3) "The journey of thousand miles begin with a single step."

– Lao Tzu

4) "If I could define enlightenment briefly, I would say it is the quiet acceptance of what is."

– Wayne Dyer

5) "If you are working on something exciting that you really care about, you don't have to be pushed. The vision pulls you."

– Steve Jobs

6) "It is in your moments of decision that your destiny is shaped."

– Tony Robbins

7) "Gratitude drives happiness. Happiness boosts productivity. Productivity reveals mastery. And mastery inspires the world."

– Robin Sharma.